salmonpoetry

*Publishing Irish & International
Poetry Since 1981*

Joan McBreen's *Map and Atlas* comes to us from a confluence of two great rivers; two streams of thought, the one private, the other public. Her mapwork has been achieved through observation and memory, through a restlessness in nature and clear-headed observations made through windows flung open. Here is a springtime of stony beaches, prairies and cities, but also a twilight where the black crow scrapes the ground, where both love and misfortune are brought to an equal poetic reckoning. In remembering the poet Jane Kenyon on All Hallows' Eve, she also invokes her lost father, but she calls both together, in memory, among the last sweet peas and peonies of the year. Standing in Katherine Mansfield's house in Wellington, New Zealand, she takes into her own work the 'shreds of a writer's life' and accepts the vocation she has also chosen as a pendant, or a gift from a brother. She awaits inspiration as she waits for swallows at the beginning of spring; waiting for that spark, that timeless instruction, both poetic and maternal, 'whose words like poems/ knock and struggle to get out.' *Map and Atlas* is, therefore, an important work of achievement and yearning. Poems like 'Whitethorn,' 'A Full Cup' and 'Ablaze in an Enamel Pail' are themselves ablaze with a clear, precise lyricism that has become a characteristic of McBreen's style over the years, but the other, darker, more meditative work is present also, in poems like 'Zürich Hauptbahnhof' and 'Cardiff, March 1995.' Here is a poet widely travelled, from Omey to Wellington, but with the lens constantly looking inward: 'The senses are not visionary/ and we ask neither more nor less/ of this earth in whose measure/ we are fixed.' *Map and Atlas* is a work of great emotional clarity and honesty, a poetry at once intimate and universal, from a poet who goes from strength to strength with every year that passes.

THOMAS MCCARTHY

Map and Atlas

Joan McBreen

Published in 2017 by
Salmon Poetry
Cliffs of Moher, County Clare, Ireland
Website: www.salmonpoetry.com
Email: info@salmonpoetry.com

Paperback ISBN 978-1-910669-82-2
Hardback ISBN 978-1-910669-95-2

COVER ILLUSTRATION & DESIGN: *Vincent Murphy @ artisanhouse.ie*
TYPESETTING: *Siobhán Hutson*
SALMON LOGO: *Joe Boske*
Printed in Ireland by Sprint Print

Salmon Poetry gratefully acknowledges the support of
The Arts Council / An Chomhairle Ealaíon

for Patrick McBreen

Acknowledgements

Acknowledgements are due to the editors of the following publications where some of the poems in this collection were published or broadcast, sometimes in different versions:

'April in Rusheenduff': *The Letterfrack Poetry Trail,* curated by Leo Hallissey with plaques designed by Conservation Letterfrack. Broadcast by Gráinne O'Malley and Mary Ruddy. Connemara Community Radio.

'Cardiff, 1995' and 'February Song': *What Writers Do*, Lenoir-Rhyne University, N.C. Visiting Writers Series edited by Rand Brandes.

'At the Grave of Kate O'Brien', 'Homage to Omey', 'Vilhelm Hammershøi', 'Spring Haiku', 'People on Trains', 'Blackberries': *New Hibernia Review*, Vol 15, No 4, Winter 2011 edited by James Silas Rogers.

'Poem after a Wedding': *The Tuam Herald*, edited by David Burke and *Windows 20 Years of Windows Publications*, edited by Noel Monahan and Heather Brett.

'Poem for All Hallows' Eve': *Thinking Continental: Writing the Planet One Place at a Time* edited by Drucilla Wall, Susan Naramore Maher, Tom Lynch and Alan Weltzien. University of Nebraska Press.

'Map and Atlas' (earlier 'The Stone Jug'): *Washing Windows? Irish Women Write Poetry* edited by Alan Hayes, Arlen House, Galway. An Arlen House 40th birthday anthology in honour of Eavan Boland and Catherine Rose.

'Homage to Omey': *The Mountain Ash in Connemara* CD recorded and mastered by Kenny Ralph. Sun Street Studios, Tuam, Co. Galway.

'Leaving Inis Meáin': *Connemara and Aran* – photography by Walter Pfeiffer, edited by Mary Ruddy (Artisan House, 2017).

Grateful thanks to Bookmark with Don Noble, Alabama Public Television for my interview broadcast 9th April, 2014: https:vimeo.com/91523381.

Thanks to Vincent Murphy, Creative Director, Artisan House Publishing, Letterfrack, Co. Galway for his cover illustration, author photograph, and map pages 12 and 13.

Special thanks to Tom McCarthy and members of the Advanced Poetry Workshop at Writers' Week, Listowel 2016 with whom some of the poems in this collection were shared in various forms.

To my son, Brian McBreen, thanks for ongoing work on my website: www.joanmcbreen.com

To my husband, Joe McBreen, without whose encouragement and patience this book would not have come into being.

To Niall MacMonagle for launching this book at Listowel Writers' Week, 2017, and for his loyal friendship and interest in my poetry and life over decades.

Gracious thanks to Jessie Lendennie and Siobhán Hutson at Salmon Poetry once again for their professionalism and support.

Thanks also to Jim Carney for his years of friendship and his work with me proofing the final text of this collection and all my previous publications.

I am deeply grateful to the following people for their generous support: Niall MacMonagle, Vincent Murphy, Mary Ruddy, Gráinne O'Malley, Des Kavanagh, Brendan Flynn, Eilish Wren, Martin Enright, Geraldine Higgins, Ronan McDonald, Ron Schuchard, Jonathan Allison, Mary Swander, Sandra Sprayberry, Jennifer Horne, Mary O'Donnell, Eilo Molloy, Gabriel Fitzmaurice, Mary Donnelly, James Silas Rogers, Meg Harper and Geraldine Mitchell.

Contents

II – The Story in Shadows

III - Voyages

Map *(noun)*
A diagrammatic representation
of an area of land or sea showing
infrastructure and physical features.

Let the heart be your compass

Maps have a unique power to chart and
graphically reveal the criss-cross of patterns
and relationships that underlie place.
The compass containing four opposing
elements, N, S, E and W, helps us to locate
order and direction, and ultimately our
own place in this universe.

Sickle Moon and Venus

The sickle moon
and Venus in a dark sky
shine on a night clearer
than we have seen this spring

Cornamona

the ache of April
in the heart

Map and Atlas

Your last morning in Tullybeg.
You came four thousand miles,
as swallows before
you have done.

Zürich Hauptbahnhof

On the street outside the metro,
musicians in long coats
and woollen hats play tunes.

Crocus
The island
still lies in the distance

Cardiff, March 1995

Suddenly, the afternoon turned cold,
the city seemed to still, the sky
darkened. Rain began to fall.

Leaving Inis Meáin
The sky, the sea, the earth, the morning.

Broken Pieces of Ourselves
chestnut trees in Letterfrack

At the Grave of Kate O'Brien (1897-1974)
In Faversham on a bitter April day,
birds fly over
the wet stones and grass.

Blackberries
My fingers reach for ripened fruit
in a lane near Ballinakill

Autumn Rain in Renvyle
Day after day it falls,
swans on the lake dip
their heads down

April in Rusheenduff
These nights in April
stars gleam over the ocean.

Homage to Omey
Aquamarine, the colour of the sea.
Nobody to say my name,
no one to listen to me.

25, Tinakori Road, Wellington, New Zealand
Thousands of miles from home
we enter an ordinary house
on a suburban Wellington street.

I

Homage to Omey

April in Rusheenduff

These nights in April
stars gleam over the ocean.

Morning after rain, yellow gorse
thickens, smothers in the ditch
wild cherry, hawthorn and frogspawn.

Yet in the undergrowth,
among snarls of weeds
and rough stones,
garlands of mountain creeper
weave their black roots.

The senses are not visionary
and we ask neither more nor less
of this earth in whose measure
we are fixed.

Autumn Rain in Renvyle

Day after day it falls,
swans on the lake dip
their heads down, move
slowly towards
their island nests.
I watch the lake
fade from darkness
to more darkness.

By evening the rain
ceases. I step outside,
check my coat for keys,
purse, shopping list;
grateful for a watery sun
that shines on late roses.

Blackberry Time on the High Road

One spoke of found things
on old Connemara gravestones.
Another silently read Ungaretti.
Then two entered, rain soaked,
joyous, mother, daughter.
You stir and strain blackberries,
picked earlier, washed clean.
Scalded jars gleam on the counter top.
If rain and mist cleared,
large windows would frame
a world without, bring it in,
allow its light over our stories.

Homage to Omey

Afternoon sun on my back,
irregular slap of water on rock,
and then, a skylark.

Fine sand blown over
the hill's top, over the lake,
swans, and the sound they make.

Aquamarine, the colour of the sea.
Nobody to say my name,
no one to listen to me.

Nothing to remember
but the currents' swell and shift
and the island itself;

again my head thrown back,
my eyes shut, clear music in the air
and the smell of sea wrack.

Poem after a Wedding

for Peter and Elaine

Summer and early morning.
The gate is open, the house empty.
I lean on the wall, suddenly cold.
Shrubby cinquefoil's five-petalled
flowers shine in the ditch.

If I were to call out your names
you might not answer.
I pull bitter vetch and spring gentians,
strewn with blown May blossom
from grass and stones.

If I were to ask gifts of you
they would only be the year's
first violets and the promise
that you will carry to me
the moon's reflection in water.

Cornamona

Banks of yellow gorse
near Cornamona
and the ache of April
in the heart.

Leaving Inis Meáin

The boat is here. Not yet light
this January morning, we shiver and wait
to board. We came to honour you, John Synge,
your many summers in this place.

Nights you listened to island talk,
days you sat on rocks until dusk.
Then you closed your book
and listened to a cricket sing.

It is named Inis Meáin, middle island.
Synge, you found it full of sweetness –
often shut against you,
sometimes wide open as the sea.

We depart at 8.10am. The sea roars
infinitely louder than in summer.
We glance back only once as you did.
The island grows smaller. We dock in Rossaveal.

Perhaps it is time to tell you
the rest of our day is expected
to be fog-bound with a blizzard
moving in from the north.

The sky, the sea, the earth, the morning.

Map and Atlas

Your last morning in Tullybeg.
You came four thousand miles,
as swallows before
you have done.

In cold rain, after you left,
I walked to Rusheenduff.
Only a handful of flowers would do —
bird's-foot trefoil, selfheal.

I put these wild flowers
of the west in a stone jug
on my windowsill. Without map
or atlas I send them to you.

Rowan Tree

Ordinary day of autumn rain.
"Look behind," you said, "look
at my tree". Branches laden
with rowan berries, dark clouds
threaten, coastal fog creeps in,
rises, falls.

That tree would have died,
ivy would strangle it,
but your bare hands tore
sinewy poisonous climbers
with shiny, five-pointed leaves
away from the bark.

O mountain ash, rowan tree,
speak of abundance, share
secret powers, for fiercer winds
come with winter
and red clusters will fall.
Your tree will survive with sadness,

near a ditch of rats in foul water.

Whitethorn

Days of mist. Whitethorn in flower
on the High Road. Green, young,
the honeysuckle at my blue door.
The Atlantic breaks on the strand.

As whitethorn falls like confetti
and mist turns to rain, I go inside.
My hands are over my eyes.
You put away the children's things.

No brave branch died last winter.
The haws endured the snow.
Whitethorns in fields and ditches
shelter blackbird, linnet and wren.

Broken Pieces of Ourselves

The chestnut leaves begin to turn.
I walk uphill on an old path.
A broken mirror catches my eye
in the undergrowth.
I take it in my hands
and see reflected in it
chestnut trees in Letterfrack.

Hazelwood

I went out to the hazel wood,
Because a fire was in my head,

W.B. Yeats

So it was that August afternoon.
Hazel trees shaded us,
their nuts a rough carpet
under our feet. Wild garlic
shimmered in the grass,
Lough Gill glittered in sunlight.

The wood was silent, a shelter
with no sense of occasion –
when dusk fell we left
and took the path back
to our other world –

birds fluttered their wings
startled themselves –
we turned for one last look
and suddenly it was childhood –
long afternoons there;

bicycles thrown against stumps
of trees, abandoned sandals,
brown feet, then a rush
to gather ourselves, go home.
Little memory of summer showers,
or foxgloves, oxeye daises gathered

for our mothers, left behind to wither, die.
August then so different. But still,
swans drift on the lake,
white necks elegant under wings.

Blackberries

My fingers reach for ripened fruit
in a lane near Ballinakill.
One by one, I drop them in a bowl
until it is heavy, dark.

Look. I stand on the earth,
the air is mild, unseen creatures
rustle in the ditch, movements
of my hand disturb their darkness.

A beam of light falls on a spider's work
which I have no desire to destroy.
You walk towards me
and add your black hoard to mine.

The church gates are locked
and the rain barrels are full —
you wash the berries, pick
them clean. The water blackens

and harsh stars appear as night falls.

Wood Pigeons

Every summer
wood pigeons
in their grey coats
and white ringed necks

fly from cedar pines
to lilac trees,
their songs louder,
coarser than other birds.

They steal the sounds
of even black crows
who fall silent
and settle down

on gable ends,
listen to trucks
and cars and shouts
of children on swings.

Wood pigeons believe
there are no rules,
think their endless
coos are worth

all there is to sing about –
perhaps they are right
and praise, love and sorrow
are a chorus to heaven

as beautiful as a violin
repeating over and over
the same notes of music
a mother sings to her child

as he enters sleep
safe under his eiderdown,
neither in need of answers
nor questions as he leaves

his day for the safety of night.

Late August Morning

Garlands of clouds,
some darker than others,
throw themselves with no mercy
on the wild flowers
in the ditch —
a thrush sits motionless
on a stone.
Over our country lane
the sky arranges itself.

Skylark

Flame red montbretia,
fading yellow honeysuckle,
last of summer's meadowsweet
rain sodden in the ditch.

Rowans bend in the wind
over graves of the dead,
sun shines and a skylark's song
reminds me of the words

I need to carry in my heart.

The Language of Poetry

Place another stone
against a jug
of montbretia and meadowsweet,
those wild flowers
of fragility and endurance.

Poem for All Hallows' Eve

i.m. Jane Kenyon

Although late October sun brightens the morning,
flowers and grass are doomed. Yesterday
leaves came down around me from arches of trees

over the road near Cong. I remembered that you, Jane,
once wrote: *diminishing light contributes to our sense
of loss*. I bring in the last of the sweet pea and peonies,

check the small, hard tomatoes in the greenhouse,
plant a few spring bulbs, and remember you, too,
my lost father, as I look again at the sepia photograph

of you, aged six, in a sailor suit, your head almost
on your sister's shoulder, your hands joined.

The Light under the Leaves

October. Dead leaves congregate
along the roadsides
under the trees. Ragged in mist
and shorter days, gusts disturb
them. They dance and fly
leaving space where sunlight
illuminates a dropped glove on stones.
At times of loss and distance
a river glitters as rivers do.

Your spade opens the earth,
a wound. Potatoes, beetroot,
carrots, onions, are lifted from the dark.
You pack them in straw, push them
under our neighbour's gate. Suddenly
the sky darkens. You turn for home.
The heart does not regret simple gifts,
even black encrusted ones.
Nor does the heart lose the memory
of leaves in the light under trees.

Crocus

Despite the cold,
purple crocus flower in pots
where two stone walls meet.
The rain is wet on the road
and all that has been left
of winter is brown grass
and burnt ferns under bare
branches of willow and thorn.

As I walk I am grateful the island
still lies in the distance,
and the mountain is lit
from behind by a weak sun.
I reach the shore and gentle waves
endlessly repeat themselves
over pebbles and sea wrack.
I am witness to spring once more.

Starlings at Curlew Cottage, Renvyle

In silence
we watch starlings
balance on wires,

then with a freedom
we will never know,
they fly in formation

over the sea.

II
The Story in Shadows

Nights

When nights
have been sleepless
the mind roams
from familiar
stony beaches,
to prairies, cities,
afflicted lives
of others, then
I wander
to a window,
and a full moon,
an evening star.

People on Trains

They pose for you,
stare out windows, belong
where they are, out of the rain.

They look at litter
blown on platforms,
at the woman and the boy

who cries for his red balloon,
flown into the last light
of a winter afternoon.

People on trains sit still,
arrange themselves
until the whistle blows.

Sickle Moon and Venus

Early evening. Here is a street.
Here are houses. The sickle moon
and Venus in a dark sky
shine on a night clearer
than we have seen this spring.

I want to knock on all the doors
and shout, "come out, come out,"
but your silent attention
to this miraculous night sky
is enough. I reach into my pocket

and give you all I have –
one smooth stone, a silver coin,
a poem about a storm scribbled
on the back of an envelope,
fixed in a rhyme, written with tears.

Spring Haiku

Frost on the grass
one bird in the bright
air. And tears.

Storm

The storm is in from the north.
It rages all night. In the morning
winter jasmine's yellow flowers
have steadfastly held here to the wall.
Spring has not abandoned us.
There are early violets in the ditch.

Lament

When they told me a bird
had been flying
in the house
I remembered my
mother's fear —
her song a lament for a death
that would soon follow.
"Close the windows"
she would sing,
her words jagged as stone.

February Song

Lift the latch, enter the room.
Stand in silence behind the woman
who writes at a table facing a window
learning what lines and shadows teach.
She knows that rain threatens
the fading light,
that you left a café
to buy her anemones,
that the world's promises
given and stolen
are not the enemy,
that you will be there
when she turns towards you,
lost in her song of grief.

Cherry Blossom on
Clonskeagh Road

First sight of cherry blossom
at the turn of the road,
an entire heaven.

Candlelight

For weeks the large candle
has been lit. Day by day
its small flame slowly
melted the wax.

Beside it she placed
a tiny bone china plate
bearing your name
printed in black

under painted violets, gentians,
irises. And spring itself
came early, its sunlight
in pools on surfaces.

In silence, the afternoon
throws its shadows
over the woman who leans
her head on her hand

and seems to dream
of day descending into night –
dreams she keeps to herself
as she blows the candle out.

Ablaze in an Enamel Pail

The enamel flower pail
you brought at Christmas
was filled with dark compost.

I placed it outside
my front door, watered
it from time to time.

The sight of green shoots
breaking through
is my reward this spring day,

and the knowledge
that soon red or purple
tulips will be in bloom.

They will stand upright
in all weathers
and the mothers passing

along the road will smile,
will point them out
to their children,

who may for one moment
leave a mongrel dog alone,
stop fighting for his attention,

gaze at the colour of flowers.

Waiting for Swallows

Another late spring day,
cold; tapers of catkins catch
the eye. Still no sign of swallows.

Rain in pearls on daffodils.
A funeral bell is heard
in the distant village.

Letters, some unanswered,
lie on a desk.
I will soon send love,

words that bear my signature
but I will not mention
that black crow scraping

the ground or on the roof
as I wait for swallows
to return, return,

as you wait for my letters,
whose words like poems
knock and struggle to get out.

The Story in Shadows

i

Always the story is in shadows.
I sit by a window. Outside, a willow.

Were my early songs out of tune,
my voice unheard?

People and things crowded in,
I allowed it, mistook all for light.

Was I wrong? Should I have embraced
silence or learned to speak truth?

I scattered memories of an unknown
world, to darkness and rain.

ii

This first day of spring, my pen
creaks across the page. I could write

of a crow on the oak branch
with his knowledge of the tree.

Instead I push the lamp aside, stare
ahead. Years have passed

faster than matchlight.
In twilight, I go outside.

iii

I kick a dead fish
along a beach, lift it with my foot.

It falls on wet sand, makes no sound.
Ebb tide in the west.

I sit on a rock, watch you walk away
around a headland.

III
Voyages

25, Tinakori Road, Wellington, New Zealand

You leave little bits of yourself
fluttering on the fences – little rags
and shreds of your very life...

Katherine Mansfield to Ida Baker
March 1922

If poems are miracles
so too are pilgrimages.

Thousands of miles from home
we enter an ordinary house
on a suburban Wellington street.

From here a dark-hearted,
short-sighted girl set sail
with her sisters for England
and school – the Antipodes
threatened to smother her,
and her stories, ones the world
would have and for which
she paid a terrible price.

In silence as we moved
from room to room,
we felt like trespassers –

looking at objects, beloved
belongings and trinkets,
letters, photographs,
books and clothing a woman
and a writer had given

to friends and lovers,
returned over years
to where they belonged.

Ida Baker wrote after her
beloved Mansfield's death in 1923:

> *...they had taken Katherine to a small chapel...*
> *I stood beside her as she lay in the light wooden*
> *coffin, and thought how cold and bare it looked.*
> *She would have hated that. So I fetched her brilliantly*
> *embroidered black silk Spanish shawl and covered her*
> *with it...I knew it was somehow right.*

And so it was for us that day
of pilgrimage, taking into ourselves
shreds of a writer's life, museum pieces.
We carried home one abiding
image – her bowenite pendant,
fashioned from clear translucent
stone, named from a Maori legend
about the tears of a lamenting woman.

The pendant, a gift from her brother,
Leslie, killed in Belgium in 1915,
was kept by Katherine, who
more often than not
wore it around her neck until her death.

At the Grave of Kate O'Brien

(1897–1974)

for Eibhear Walshe

In Faversham on a bitter April day,
birds fly over
the wet stones and grass.
Three times we walk among the paths
and graves and cannot find yours.

Is your only need now the sway of trees
and secret meetings with tufts of time?
But we have travelled far to leave here
without bringing you one spray
of thyme and mock orange blossom.

A sudden downpour, pierced
by shafts of sleet. We stumble
on your headstone. It leans to one side
in all its brokenness.
One crow flies into the sky.

Cardiff, March 1995

Suddenly, the afternoon turned cold,
the city seemed to still, the sky
darkened. Rain began to fall.

The peaches in her bag were ripe.
She had bought them cheap.
Nonetheless they tasted good.

He came towards her along the street,
holding irises and roses
wrapped in white paper.

She took them from him.
In her left hand were the peaches,
in her right she held the flowers.

She could not wipe the rain
or tears from her face.

Scented Stock

The purple scented stock
stands in cut glass
on the kitchen counter.

The room is deserted.
Rain beats on windows
at the edge of the Atlantic.

Far away, soldiers
fight their fights,
cross mountains, borders,

into marshy meadows
where poppies grow,
arrive in villages

where men and women
warm their hands at fires
or point at the sky

yearning for the scent
of flowers whose names
they have forgotten.

Vilhelm Hammershøi:
The Poetry of Silence

(The Royal Academy, 2008)

The empty interiors
disturbed only by a solitary figure,
the painter's wife.

We gaze at her back, graceful,
wearing white and grey,
her long white neck exposed, hair upswept.

One door in the house leads into another.
In painting after painting, the rooms
are haunted.

Nothing and everything to be said –
we brought the noise of the city
streets in with us

and left with the painter's poetry
of silence. We bought white flowers then,
against the heartbreak of survival.

Zürich Hauptbahnhof

On the street outside the metro,
musicians in long coats
and woollen hats play tunes.
Even a dog listens, ears cocked.
The guitarist stops play
and shakes his box
above the noise
of ceaseless traffic.

We run past
to catch our train,
then regret the coins
we did not throw,
for one tune remained
in our heads all day –
an old stubborn one
my mother played
years ago on her piano
in our house in Sligo.

Sometimes she sang
the words too –
Roses are shining
in Picardy. Little wonder
the cemetery where she lies
is full of silences. Yet
with her ghost there,
that time comes again and again.

Azinhaga, Portugal

i.m. José Saramago (1922-2010)

i

Here, José, you were born
in this village, whose name
means narrow street.

Although aged only two
when you were carried off
to Lisbon, you sent down roots

for your fragile, unsteady feet,
into clay, dry and wet
to know or not then know

that one day you would return
to Azinhaga to 'finish being born'.
In time you would write

for good or ill, what you alone
made of your secret, solitary self
when, as a child, you were simply

in the landscape, never seeing it
as the man you would become
when you absorbed it into your spirit.

ii

In the square, if it could be called a square,
there is a seated image of you cast
in bronze, under an oak tree.

Children had filled your outstretched hand
with acorns. As we leave we think of you
letting yourself be led by the child you were.

iii

Only you, in 1998, could open your Nobel lecture
with the words: 'The wisest man I ever knew
in my whole life could not read or write'.

Your grandfather, that wise man, carried weakling
piglets from the sty to his marital bed,
saving them from freezing death,

not out of compassion but to protect his family's
daily bread. So, from your early novel
Raised from the Ground you wrote of your own

people, who did not think about more than was needful.
And later, in novel after novel, José, you wrote
like a fine old apple tree, heavily laden with fruit.

You remind us that everything can be remembered,
connected, spoken of and taught to speak,
but above all, can and should be written down.

JOAN MCBREEN is from Sligo. She divides her time between Tuam and Renvyle, County Galway. Her poetry collections are: *The Wind Beyond the Wall* (Story Line Press, 1990), *A Walled Garden in Moylough* (Story Line Press and Salmon Poetry, 1995), *Winter in the Eye — New and Selected Poems* (Salmon Poetry, 2003) and *Heather Island* (Salmon Poetry, 2009; reprinted 2013 & 2016). She was awarded an MA from University College, Dublin in 1997. Her anthology *The White Page / An Bhileog Bhán — Twentieth-Century Irish Women Poets* was published by Salmon in 1999 and is in its third reprint. She also edited and compiled the anthology *The Watchful Heart — A New Generation of Irish Poets — Poems and Essays* (Salmon, 2009).

Her poetry is published widely in Ireland and abroad and has been broadcast, anthologised and translated into many languages. Her CD *The Long Light on the Land — Selected Poems*, read to a background of traditional Irish airs and classical music, was produced by Ernest Lyons Productions, Castlebar, County Mayo in 2004. Her most recent CD is *The Mountain Ash in Connemara — Selected Poems by Joan McBreen*, read by the poet to new arrangements of Irish airs and original music by composer Glen Austin, performed by the RTÉ Contempo Quartet. 2015 saw the publication of a limited edition broadside, *The Mountain Ash*, with an original etching by the artist Margaret Irwin West alongside Joan McBreen's poem, 'The Mountain Ash'. Set in letterpress and hand-printed by Mary Plunkett of the Belgrave Private Press, Dublin. Published by Artisan House, Connemara. 150 copies signed by artist and poet, numbered and dated.

She has given readings and talks in many universities in the USA including Emory, Villanova, de Paul (Chicago), Cleveland, Lenoir Rhyne, N.C. and the University of Missouri - St. Louis. In 2010 she undertook a six week reading tour of Nebraska, Iowa and Alabama and in 2012 she read at the University of St. Thomas, St. Paul, MN and at the University of Minnesota, Duluth. Her most recent US reading was at the 2017 American Conference of Irish Studies (ACIS South), University of Kentucky, Lexington.

Joan McBreen has been involved for many years with Irish literary festivals such as the Yeats International Summer School, Clifden Arts Week, Listowel Writers' Week and the Cúirt International Festival of Literature, Galway. She is also a member of the Board of Poetry Ireland.

www.joanmcbreen.com

BY THE SAME AUTHOR

POETRY
The Wind Beyond the Wall
Story Line Press, Oregon, 1990, reprinted 1991

A Walled Garden in Moylough
Story Line Press, Oregon and Salmon Poetry, Co. Clare, 1995

Winter in the Eye — New and Selected Poems
Salmon Poetry, Co. Clare, 2003

Heather Island
Salmon Poetry, Co. Clare, 2009, reprinted 2013 and 2016

AS EDITOR
The White Page - An Bhileog Bhán: Twentieth-Century Irish Women Poets.
Salmon Poetry, Co. Clare, 1999, reprinted 2000, 2001, 2007 (anthology)

The Watchful Heart — A New Generation of Irish Poets — Poems and Essays. Salmon Poetry, Co. Clare, 2009 (anthology)

CDs
The Long Light on the Land — Selected Poems: read to a background of traditional Irish airs and classical music.
Ernest Lyons Productions, Cloondeash, Castlebar, Co. Mayo, 2004

The Mountain Ash in Connemara — Selected Poems by Joan McBreen, read by the poet to new arrangements of Irish airs and original music by composer Glen Austin. Performed by the RTÉ Contempo Quartet.
Recorded and mastered by Kenny Ralph, Sun Street Studios, Tuam, Co. Galway, 2014

BROADSIDE
The Mountain Ash. Limited Edition Broadside with an original etching by the artist Margaret Irwin West alongside Joan McBreen's poem, 'The Mountain Ash'. Set in letterpress and hand-printed by Mary Plunkett of The Belgrave Private Press, Dublin. Published by Artisan House, Connemara. 150 copies signed by artist and poet, numbered and dated.